A Good Read

A Guide to Twenty-one Authors

Written by Chris Lutrario

Collins Educational
An imprint of HarperCollinsPublishers

Contents

Introduction	3
Joan Aiken	4/5
Chris van Allsburg	6/7
Bernard Ashley	8/9
Raymond Briggs	10/11
Betsy Byars	12/13
Gillian Cross	14/15
Anne Fine	16/17
Nicholas Fisk	18/19
Leon Garfield	20/21
Adèle Geras	22/23
Morris Gleitzman	24/25
Gene Kemp	26/27
Dick King-Smith	28/29
Robert Leeson	30/31
Jan Mark	32/33
Graham Oakley	34/35
Philippa Pearce	36/37
Phillip Ridley	38/39
Jon Scieszka	40/41
Jill Paton Walsh	42/43
Jacqueline Wilson	44/45
Title index	46/47
Finding out more	48

Introduction

Do you sometimes feel like a 'good read' but don't know what to choose or where to go for information? If so, this book will help. It offers information about the life and work of twenty-one well-known and important authors of children's fiction. Each author has her or his own special way of looking at the world, of telling a story, of using words.

Some of the books in *A Good Read* will make you laugh. Some will make you think – about yourself, or about other people, other places, other times. Some will take you into a world of fantasy or make believe. There are some books to relax with; there are also books which present a real challenge in terms of both subject matter and style.

A Good Read will help you to find the kinds of books you know you like. But it will also tempt you to try reading something new and different.

The world is full of wonderful books, so don't forget that this is only a small selection. These authors have written other books and there are many other authors.

Happy reading!

Joan Aiken

Joan Aiken, the daughter of the American poet Conrad Aiken, was born in Rye in East Sussex in 1924. She began writing stories and poems in her late teens. Before taking up writing as a full-time career in 1960, she worked as an editor on the literary magazine, *Argosy*, as a copywriter for an advertising agency, and for the United Nations. She writes fiction for adults as well as children.

The Wolves of Willoughby Chase (1962)

Joan Aiken is most famous for the long and enthralling series of historical fantasies which begins with *The Wolves of Willoughby Chase*. These novels are set in a period of English history which never actually existed: the reign of a James III. It is a time when the most unlikely things are happening: air balloons, castles, trains, and guns which can fire across the Atlantic Ocean exist side by side. Wolves come into England through the newly-opened Channel Tunnel. The books are full of action, adventure and intrigue. More than that, though, they create a whole new world peopled by extraordinary characters: evil governesses, long-lost children, witches, scheming politicians, smugglers, kidnappers and every other kind of villain you could imagine. Holding this all together are two heroes, Simon and Dido Twite. The style of the stories is as rich and fullblooded as the events they relate.

Each of the novels is complete in itself, but they also follow on from one another to form one long story. So read them in this order, if you can: *The Wolves of Willoughby Chase*; *Black Hearts in Battersea* (1965); *Night Birds on Nantucket* (1966); *The Stolen Lake* (1981); *The Cuckoo Tree* (1971); *Dido and Pa* (1986); *Is* (1992) and *Cold Shoulder Road* (1995).

Joan Aiken

Go Saddle the Sea (1978)

Twelve year old Felix escapes from a lonely existence in his grandfather's great house in Spain to find his father's family in England. On his journey across Europe he encounters many hardships and adventures, including wolves, floods, storms, duels and imprisonment.

This is the first book in *The Felix Brooke Trilogy*, a series of long novels in which the author describes places and people in vivid detail. Yet, at the same time, the plot keeps moving, there is plenty of incident and adventure, and a huge cast of larger-than-life characters. The other two titles are *Bridle the Wind* (1983) and *The Teeth of the Gale* (1988).

As well as these series of novels, Joan Aiken has also written many collections of short stories, including the following:

A Harp of Fishbones (1972)

This is a challenging, varied and richly imaginative collection of fourteen stories, mostly about magic and fantasy. Some are humorous, some mysterious, some atmospheric. In them you will meet princesses, witches, mermaids, dragons, demons... but not always quite in the form you would expect.

Tales of Mystery

Every few years, Joan Aiken publishes a collection of scary, spooky stories. The wonderful titles give you the idea: *A Bundle of Nerves* (1976); *A Whisper in the Night* (1982); *A Touch of Chill* (1979); *A Creepy Company* (1995); *A Goose on Your Grave* (1987); *A Fit of Shivers* (1992). The strange, supernatural happenings in these stories are all the more believable because of the detailed, realistic settings which Joan Aiken creates. Many of them explore interesting ideas, like the nature of dreams and hauntings. These are mysterious, disturbing stories, full of shocks and puzzles, suspense and flashes of macabre humour. You will not want to stop reading until you get to the end!

Chris van Allsburg

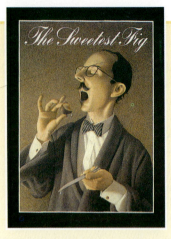

Chris van Allsburg is an American artist and sculptor who also writes and illustrates books for children.

In his outstandingly beautiful books, he illustrates in full colour, black and white and sepia. His soft delicate pictures, with their striking effects of light and shade, create an enchanting dream-like world where the reader is never quite sure of what is happening, or why.

The Wreck of the Zephyr (1983)

The mystery in this story concerns how the Zephyr, a small sail boat, came to be wrecked on top of the cliffs. Was it simply the result of a freak storm? Or was it, as the old man explains in a story within the story, because a boy who owned this boat learned to sail it not on the water but through the air above it? The still, magical pictures in this book make us believe in the possibility of such journeys.

The Mysteries of Harris Burdick (1984)

Harris Burdick turned up at a publisher's office with samples of his work: one soft, grainy, black and white illustration, with a caption, for each of fourteen stories. Then he disappeared, and was never heard from again. So this book contains all that we have of his work. But what is happening in the pictures? And what could the stories from which they come have been about? An original and fascinating book in which each page provides the starting point for a flight of fancy – where the reader has to do most of the work!

Chris van Allsburg

The Polar Express (1985)

One Christmas Eve, a boy lies awake hoping to hear the sound of the bells on Santa's sleigh. Instead, he hears the hissing of a steam train, the Polar Express, as it stops outside his house. The train takes him and all the other children on board to a great city 'where every Christmas toy was made,' and where Santa Claus chooses the boy to receive the very first gift of the season. A solemn, atmospheric story which makes the reader think about what it means to believe in something.

The Widow's Broom (1992)

It is no ordinary broom that the widow finds in her pumpkin patch. It is a witch's broom that has fallen from the sky. It is still powerful enough to help with the housework ('Sweeping brought it special pleasure. It was after all, a broom') and to play the piano. But, seeing it at work, the widow's neighbours, including the children, think it is wicked, and set out to destroy it. This is a powerful, thought-provoking story about the way in which people react to things that are new and strange. The sepia illustrations are full of spooky shadows, and the whole book is beautifully designed and in an unusual tall, thin shape.

The Sweetest Fig (1994)

A poor woman has no money with which to pay the dentist, Monsieur Bibot. Instead, she gives him two figs which, she says, will make his dreams come true. That night he dreams of taking his dog out for a walk in his underwear – and wakes to find that this is just what he is doing. He sets out to put the remaining fig to better use: to make himself rich. However, his attempts are frustrated by the dog, which has other dreams to fulfil.
A sophisticated story with surreal illustrations.

Bernard Ashley

Bernard Ashley lives and works in south-east London, where he was born in 1935. He is the head teacher of Charlton Manor Junior School. He has written novels and collections of short stories for a wide age range, from young children to teenagers. Several of his novels have been made into television drama series. These include *Terry on the Fence* and *Break in the Sun*, for which he wrote the script himself. His son, Chris, is also an author, and they have collaborated on a book of stories.

Bernard Ashley's stories combine fast, exciting action with thought-provoking ideas and interesting, complex characters. They have a strong sense of place and of community life.

Terry on the Fence (1975)

After a row at home Terry runs off, gets involved with Les and his gang, and is forced to break into his own school to steal radios and tape-recorders. He gets caught, and in trying to sort things out, finds himself facing difficult moral choices. This is a hard-hitting, realistic novel which offers adventure and lots of issues to think about. The long chapters are divided into short episodes to show how the action shifts from one character or scene to another.

Break in the Sun (1980)

This story also involves running away from home. Patsy, mistreated by her mother's new husband Eddie, runs off with a touring theatre group who are sailing down the Thames and round the coast of Kent on a barge. Eddie, accompanied by Patsy's friend Kenny, sets off to find her and bring her back. There is lots of action in this story, but even more striking and interesting are the characters. Children and adults alike are portrayed with great depth and subtlety, and the reader begins to understand and feel sympathy for all of them, even the apparently horrid Eddie. There are no easy answers as the book reaches its powerful and unusually open-ended conclusion.

Bernard Ashley

I'm Trying to Tell You (1981)

Bernard Ashley writes that 'the children of Saffin Street School, like all of us, have their stories to tell', and this book consists of four of them – each told in a different way. For example, Nerissa's story about her sister's wedding is told as a monologue in her own conversational voice. Lyn is away on a school journey, and her story comes in the form of two series of letters: one written to her parents, telling the polite, official version of events; the other to her sister, telling the ruder, unofficial version. Don't be put off by the fact that this book is a Picture Puffin, a series intended for young children: it is an intriguing collection.

Dockside School stories

A series of four short illustrated novels featuring the children and adults involved in one way or another with Dockside School: *Boat Girl*, *The Ghost of Dockside School*, *The Caretaker's Cat* and *Getting In*. Although very accessible, these stories are not as simple as they might first appear. They have a very realistic, up-to-date tone, and provide a rich mixture of action, characters and issues. The books are full of sharp, detailed observation: 'Kenny met his stare, tried to look a mix of innocent and cheeky, did a little angle of his head like Granddad had in the bedroom.'

Seeing Off Uncle Jack (1991)

Two long stories about the members of the Stone family. The title story is set at the time of blind Uncle Jack's funeral, and explores the very different reactions of brother and sister, Winnie and Danny. The second story, 'The Princess Watch', centres on Winnie's attempt to get her precious watch repaired without her parents finding out that she has damaged it. These are sensitive and good-natured stories which take a long, close look at just one simple event.

Raymond Briggs

Raymond Briggs, the author and illustrator of many popular, imaginative and thought-provoking picture books, was born in London in 1934. He went to the Wimbledon and Slade Schools of Art, and began illustrating children's books while still a student.

He has developed a distinctive visual style based on the comic-strip, but expanding its possibilities. His books combine the (sometimes rude) details of everyday life with a sense of magic. They are endlessly inventive and amusing, but often also involve challenging ideas about identity, and the relationship between fantasy and reality.

Father Christmas books (1973)

Raymond Briggs' own distinctive style was first displayed in *Father Christmas* and *Father Christmas Goes on Holiday*. These bring the make-believe character to life as a rather ill-tempered old man who complains about 'blooming snow', 'blooming chimneys' and 'blooming Christmas'. Although usually thought of as books for young children, the witty, detailed pictures and sheer sense of fun also have a lot to offer older readers.

Fungus the Bogeyman (1977)

One of the rudest and most subversive books ever created, *Fungus the Bogeyman* is altogether a more challenging and sophisticated book. It is not so much a story as an encyclopedia of life in Bogeydom, a place where everything that human beings find disgusting is loved and admired. Bogeymen and Bogeywomen change their sheets when the dirt begins to wear *off*, use toothpaste that makes their teeth black, and keep their clothes in tanks of cold water. The pictures are packed with detail and there are lots of all-too-informative speech bubbles, labels and captions. Not for the squeamish!

Raymond Briggs

The Snowman (1978)

The magical, gentle world of *The Snowman* could hardly be more different from Bogeydom. The story is now better known as a cartoon film, shown every Christmas on television, than as a book. A boy builds a snowman that comes to life during the night, explores the boy's house, and flies around the sky with him. (Notice that this episode is much shorter than in the film.) When the boy wakes up after these adventures, he rushes downstairs to find that the snowman has melted. This is a wordless picture book: look at it and make up the story for yourself!

Gentleman Jim (1980)

Here, Raymond Briggs returns to a more earthy subject. This book tells the sad story of a lavatory attendant who wants a more exciting life. He imagines all sorts of possibilities – commando, tail-gunner, artist, executive, cowboy... Finally he decides to become a highwayman, but ends up in jail and eventually back in his old job, sadder, perhaps wiser, but certainly with his optimism and sense of adventure still intact. Although very funny, this is not a light-hearted book. It looks at the dangers of confusing fact with fantasy, and at the way in which those in authority treat, or mistreat, other people. Along the way, the author has lots of fun using different styles of writing.

The Man (1992)

Imagine waking up one morning and finding a tiny man on your bedside table. This is the starting point of *The Man*. Being so small, the Man cannot cope with life in the human world – a predicament that makes him rather irritable and aggressive. He persuades (or perhaps forces) the boy who discovers him to help him with finding food and drink, keeping clean, and with many other aspects of life both necessary and not so necessary: the Man likes his comforts. This funny, unsettling story describes the problems the Man and the boy face and (usually) overcome, and the ups and downs of their relationship. It makes the reader think again about little ordinary details of our lives that we take for granted. The text takes the form of a dialogue between the boy and the Man, set out rather like a play script.

Betsy Byars

Betsy Byars was born in North Carolina, USA, in 1928. She began her career by writing articles for newspapers and magazines while at home looking after her two children. As they grew up, she wrote stories for them to read. She is a licensed pilot, and spends much of her leisure time flying. She writes in a log cabin in the woods near her home.

Many of her humorous yet sensitive novels are based on her own experiences.

The Summer of the Swans (1970)

Fourteen-year-old Sara worries about the way she looks (especially the size of her feet), and it's spoiling her summer. One day she takes her younger brother, Charlie, who has a learning difficulty, to see the swans that have settled on a nearby lake. Captivated by them, he has to be dragged away. Unable to sleep that night, Charlie sets out for the lake, but gets lost. In the panicky, suspense-filled search to find him, Sara forgets her own worries and begins to realise what it is to think and care about someone else. A quiet, thoughtful novel centred on emotions and relationships.

The Midnight Fox (1970)

When Tom's parents go to Europe, they leave him with his aunt and uncle on their farm. Resentful and bored at first, life takes on new interest for Tom when he sees a black fox and discovers its den. When the fox is blamed for taking a turkey, Uncle Fred decides to kill it – and Tom tries to stop him. An exciting adventure and a perceptive picture of growing up, the story is told in the first person by Tom himself, and the reader has a clear insight into his thoughts and feelings.

Betsy Byars

The Eighteenth Emergency (1973)

Benjie – Mouse to his friends – writes the name of the school bully on a poster showing a Neanderthal man. Unfortunately, the bully is standing right behind him. While waiting for the beating up that he knows will come, Benjie imagines other emergencies (for example, Number 7: Capture by a gorilla; Number 11: Attack by a werewolf) and overcomes them all. However, there is no escaping the real emergency, which he finally has to face up to. This novel has a believable, likeable central character, and offers both humour and suspense.

The Computer Nut (1983)

One day Kate draws a picture on her father's computer, and gives it the title *Self-portrait of a computer nut*. Messages start coming through on the computer from something identifying itself as BB9. Is it an alien? Or is it all a practical joke? Kate and her friend Linda do all sorts of crazy things to find out. You don't have to be a computer nut yourself to enjoy this clever, intriguing novel. The book has an unusual appearance, with text in different styles and pictures in the style of computer graphics.

Coast to Coast (1992)

Betsy Byars draws on her love and knowledge of flying in this subtle adventure story. Birch and her grandfather have always planned secret missions together, but this is the big one: to fly across the United States from coast to coast in a small plane.

The journey has a very special meaning for each of them. The book features sharply observed family relationships and evocative descriptions of flying.

The Blossom Family Library

In this series of four linked stories, Betsy Byars introduces us to the members of a truly extraordinary family. The first book, *The Not-just-anybody Family*, lives up to its title when Vern and Maggie break into jail to visit their grandfather. The *Blossoms Meet the Vulture Lady* while trying to catch a coyote. In *The Blossoms and the Green Phantom*, Junior's home-made spaceship falls out of the sky into a neighbour's chicken shed. In *A Blossom Promise*, Maggie's mother vows to give up riding in rodeos. These immensely entertaining books, organised in very short chapters, are full of keen observation, witty language and extraordinary incidents.

Gillian Cross

Gillian Cross was born on Christmas Eve in 1945, in Wembley, north London. She studied English literature at the universities of Oxford and Sussex, and worked in various jobs, including school book club organiser, baker, and assistant to a Member of Parliament. She is married, has four children, and lives near Coventry. Her hobbies are playing the piano, long distance walking and orienteering.

Clipper, Spag and Barny series

A series of four lively, humorous books about the adventures of three friends at Bennet School. In the first, *Save our School* (1981), Clipper, Spag and Barny think up all sorts of plans to save their school from closure, including chaining themselves to the pipes and writing to the Queen. But all their plans go wrong and the school seems doomed – until one of the friends turns out to have unexpected artistic talent.

The Mintyglo Kid (1983) finds the gang struggling to survive the visit of Spag's cousin, Dreadful Denzil, who thinks he is Batman and wreaks havoc with his five-year supply of Mintyglo toothpaste.

In *Gobbo the Great* (1991) the trio celebrate the one-hundredth anniversary of their school by organising an exhibition about the future. And, in the process, they succeed in outdoing the rival local school.

Swimathon (1986) is the story of the friends' attempts to raise money for the repair of the school minibus. Again this involves competition with their dreaded rivals, Kings Road School.

These stories are packed with amusing incidents and characters, and the witty, often sarcastic dialogue is a delight.

Gillian Cross

The Demon Headmaster (1982)

Dinah is puzzled and worried by the atmosphere at her new school. Why are the children so neat and well-behaved? Why do they work right through their play-times? The cause of this unnatural state of affairs is the Demon Headmaster, who exercises mysterious and complete control over the children. As Dinah also discovers, his ambitions are not confined to the school: he aims to take over the world. With a few other children who are also immune to his powers, she forms SPLAT (Society for the Protection of our Lives Against Them), and sets out to stop him. An exciting yet amusing thriller, with some very tense moments. The Headmaster is a truly sinister creation. This novel was followed by two sequels, *The Prime Minister's Brain* and *The Revenge of the Demon Headmaster*.

The Prime Minister's Brain (1985)

All the children are trying to solve an addictive new computer game called Octopus Dare. Dinah is the only one to succeed, and so enters the Junior Computer Brain of the Year Competition. She soon realises that the powerful new Super Saladin computers used in the competition are trying to control her and the other competitors. The Demon Headmaster is behind it all – and again the fate of the world is at stake.

The Great Elephant Chase (1992)

On an errand to the shops, fifteen-year-old Tad stops to watch Michael Keenan's Great Elephant Show parading by. It is the start of a great adventure, as he becomes involved with the show. He ends up travelling with an elephant halfway across the continent, chased by the cruel, greedy Hannibal Jackson who will do anything to get his hands on the animal. An exciting and unusual adventure story, vividly set in America at the end of the nineteenth century.

The Revenge of the Demon Headmaster (1994)

Tireless in his attempts to rule the world, the Demon Headmaster creates a television programme featuring a pig called Hunky Parker. The programme exerts a strange, compelling fascination, and soon every child in the country is wearing the T-shirt and chanting the slogans – except Dinah. This novel offers a mixture of thrills, suspense and fun, and has a sharp message about the power of mass media. (Note that the title of the hardback edition of this story is *Hunky Parker Is Watching You*.)

Anne Fine

Anne Fine was born and educated in the Midlands, and studied history and politics at the University of Warwick. She began writing her first book while trapped inside her flat during snowy weather. She has two daughters, and lives in a village in County Durham.

Anne Fine has become one of the most popular and important children's authors of the past decade. *Madame Doubtfire*, her novel for older children, was made into the hit film *Mrs Doubtfire*, and *Goggle-Eyes* was adapted for television.

Crummy Mummy and Me (1988)

Anne Fine has lots of fun swapping normal roles in this amusing and eccentric book. Though still a child, Minna sees herself (with reason) as the only person in her family with any sense. This is the story, told in her own words, of her attempts to keep the family in check. For example, she tries to persuade her mother, who has bright blue hair, to dress more sensibly for a school visit, to buy healthier food, and to choose more suitable boyfriends. The current one, Crusher Maggot, is a nightmare!

Goggle-Eyes (1989)

When Helly Johnston runs in tears from the classroom, her teacher sends Kitty Killin to talk with her. The teacher knows that they share a problem: their mothers' new boyfriends. Most of this book consists of the story Kitty tells Helly while the two of them are shut up in the lost property cupboard, how she tried to upset the relationship between her mother and Gerald Faulkner, or Goggle-Eyes, as Kitty calls him. Like most of Anne Fine's novels, *Goggle-Eyes* deals realistically and forcefully with strong emotions, yet is very funny. It won the Carnegie Medal in 1990.

Anne Fine

Flour Babies (1992)

The unruly boys of 4C are not trusted with interesting, exciting science projects involving explosions or maggots. Instead, much to their disgust, they are stuck with a project on child development. Each boy is given a small sack of flour dressed in babies' clothes, and a list of rules for looking after it. For example, these flour babies must never be left unattended; they must be kept clean and dry; they must not lose weight. Thoughts of showering the classroom with flour soon disappear as the boys, unexpectedly led by the chief troublemaker of the class, Simon Martin, begin to take their responsibilities seriously. Each flour baby begins to take on a different personality. The boys cope with the stresses and strains of parenthood in different ways. The project makes them all, and especially Simon Martin, think about their own childhoods and their adult lives that lie ahead.

This is a funny, challenging and moving book about a subject that is not often touched on in books for children. It won the Carnegie Medal and the Whitbread Award.

The Angel of Nitshill Road (1992)

Celeste, the new girl at Nitshill Road School, seems too perfect to be real. She is extremely clever and well-behaved, and always speaks in elegant and correct sentences. And indeed she is not real: she is the Recording Angel sent down to Earth to sort out the bully who is making Penny, Mark and Marigold so miserable. She sets about this task in an inventive and effective way. A delightful, amusing short novel, with some perceptive things to say about bullying and how to put a stop to it.

Step by Wicked Step (1995)

Five children and their teacher, off on a school journey, arrive at a gloomy old house late at night and in the middle of a thunderstorm. Settling down in the tower room, they find an old handwritten book. On the cover are the words 'Richard Clayton Harwick. My Story. Read and Weep'. It turns out to have been written by a boy who lived in the house a long time ago, and tells of how he was cruelly treated by his stepfather. As the children take it in turns to read the story aloud to each other, they realise what they have in common: they are all part of a stepfamily. They spend the rest of the night telling each other about their very varied, and by no means all gloomy, experiences as stepchildren.

A fascinating novel in which several stories are woven together: Richard Clayton Harwick's story; the five stories the children tell; and the story of their night in the tower.

Nicholas Fisk

Nicholas Fisk is one of most important and successful writers of science fiction for children, having published over thirty books in this genre. Before becoming an author, he worked as an actor, and then in journalism, television and film. He lives in Hertfordshire with his wife Dorothy and their four children.

His stories combine adventure with thought-provoking ideas about how our society might be in the future and about other imagined worlds.

Grinny (1973)

This is a powerful, thrilling, disturbing novel, told through the entries which Timothy makes in his diary as events unfold. One day, a woman claiming to be Great Aunt Emma turns up on the Carpenter's doorstep. The adults in the family accept and welcome her, but the children are not so sure. They become increasingly suspicious – not surprisingly, as Great Aunt Emma, or Grinny as they call her, never feels cold or tired, shines in the dark, and has skin that never changes colour. And what is that strange, torch-like instrument that she keeps in her pocket? The story develops into a tense and violent struggle as the children reveal her identity.

Monster Maker (1979)

Chancy Balogh, who designs and makes monsters for sci-fi and horror films, is working on some reptile-like creatures called Slurks. He agrees to let Matt, his greatest fan, help him in his studio. Matt becomes obsessed by these creatures, and begins to wonder whether they are real. His question is answered one night when hooligans break into the studio and the monsters come to life – or do they? A short but powerful novel which leaves the reader wondering what is real and what is not.

Nicholas Fisk

A Rag, a Bone and a Hank of Hair (1980)

As the result of a nuclear accident, so few children are being born that the human race is threatened with extinction. In an attempt to prevent this, scientists have used DNA to create replica human beings of the 1940s, called Reborns. The problem is that no-one knows just how they are going to behave. Twelve-year-old Brin is given the task of introducing them to their new world. However, it is he who does the learning as they introduce him to the world of the 1940s. He begins to care about them and to rebel against his own society. This is an intriguing, complex novel which prompts us to think about possible future worlds and about what it means to be human.

Backlash (1988)

This book takes us into an even stranger world. Marooned on the planet Argosy IV, three children are being hunted down by robots called Droops. While on the run, they meet Hansi and Madrigal, who turn out to be the inventors of these Droops. Originally designed to perform household chores, the robots have driven their creators underground and developed their own extraordinary society. Indeed, they want the children as entertainment for their beautiful but cruel princess. This fast-moving adventure provides an unusual mixture of the comic and the sinister.

The Talking Car (1988)

This is an altogether lighter and more amusing story in which the central character is… a car. Programmed to say such things as, 'kindly fasten your seat belt', it has somehow acquired the ability to hold long conversations, and even developed its own rather grumpy and resentful personality. The car talks to Rob, but what will happen when it is sold to someone else?

Broops! Down the Chimney (1992)

Broops is an 'alien blob' which, one night, falls down the chimney of James's house. A series of hilarious incidents follow as the innocent and enthusiastic blob tries to make sense of various aspects of life on Earth, including school, jokes and sports. Its most entertaining and satisfying encounter is with the school bully. This is a short, light-hearted and very funny novel, yet it makes the reader think about things that are usually taken for granted.

Leon Garfield

Leon Garfield is recognised as one of the most important authors of children's books in the period since the Second World War. He was born in 1921 in Brighton, a town which features in some of his stories. On leaving school, he became an art student, but abandoned his training to serve in the Medical Corps during the Second World War. He then worked as a medical technician before taking up writing full time in 1966.

Most of his stories are set in a vividly described past. Their plots are exuberant and his writing is packed with vivid, arresting images.

Black Jack (1968)

This novel is full of larger-than-life characters – literally so in the case of Black Jack himself, the enormous thief who survives his own execution and then escapes, forcing innocent young Bartholomew Dorking to accompany him. A strange but close bond forms between this ill-matched couple during their search for safety, as they meet up with a travelling circus and rescue a girl wrongly locked up in a madhouse. A powerful, atmospheric story, full of rough, often violent, action and suspense. It is densely and vividly written; the supposed corpse of Black Jack is taken in a coffin to a house that 'looked like a coffin itself, with, maybe, another house dead inside it'.

The Apprentices (1982)

This challenging book brings together twelve stories which Leon Garfield wrote between 1976 and 1978. Set in London at the end of the eighteenth century, they centre on the lives of young apprentices (a lamplighter, a midwife, a basket-maker, an undertaker...) and take us through the course of a year, month by month, starting in October. Together they provide a wonderful gallery of characters and an unforgettably vivid picture of life 200 years ago. The stories were originally published as separate books, with beautiful illustrations by Faith Jacques. It is worth looking out for these in libraries.

Leon Garfield

Blewcoat Boy (1988)

This short novel is set in Victorian London, where Young Nick and his sister Jubilee are living on the streets, on their wits, and on their own. Young Nick is determined that they should better themselves. The first step in his plan involves obtaining a place in a school, but to do this they have first to find a father. The story is full of humour and incident, and has a satisfyingly happy ending. *Blewcoat Boy* is one of a series of stories by children's authors inspired by buildings owned by the National Trust. In this case, the building is the Blewcoat School in Westminster, which was founded in 1709 by William Green, a local brewer, to provide an education for the children of poor families.

As well as these and many other original stories, Leon Garfield's work also includes retellings of myths and legends:

King Nimrod's Tower
The Writing on the Wall
The King in the Garden

In these picture books, Leon Garfield retells three well-known stories from the Bible in a down-to-earth style which brings the characters to life while losing nothing of the power and mystery of the originals. He also introduces some new characters: for example, a boy and his badly behaved dog feature in *King Nimrod's Tower*. As usual, the style is rhythmic, inventive and full of vivid turns of phrase: 'The workmen toiled in the clouds. Eagles stole their sandwiches and rainbows painted their shirts.' The large, brilliantly coloured illustrations by Michael Bragg match the text perfectly.

The God Beneath the Sea
The Golden Shadow (1970)

Leon Garfield collaborated with the poet Edward Blishen on these challenging versions of Greek myths and legends. The style is modern and poetic, and the stories are linked almost as in a novel. *The God Beneath the Sea* consists of stories about the creation of the world and the gods; The stories in *The Golden Shadow* are of legends of the Greek heroes.

Adèle Geras

Adèle Geras was born in Jerusalem, but spent her childhood in several different countries, including Borneo and Gambia. After studying at Oxford University, she worked as a singer and actress, and taught French. She now lives in Manchester. As well as books for children, she has written a series of school stories for teenagers.

Adèle Geras's stories are about families: about their histories and the importance of maintaining links between generations. In many of her books, photographs have an important role to play in keeping family memories alive.

The Girls in the Velvet Frame (1978)

This story is set in Jerusalem in 1913 to 1914. Sarah and her five daughters are waiting anxiously for news of Isaac, who has emigrated to America. The girls decide to have their photograph taken (a very special event in those days) as a present for their mother. One of them has the idea of sending a copy to Isaac. But how will they get it to him? And will he reply? A richly descriptive, slow-moving book which evokes the sights, sounds and smells of another time and place. The story is partly told through letters between the various characters.

Voyage (1983)

It is 1904. The Isaacs family are fleeing from persecution in Europe to a new life in America. The whole of the action takes place during their two-week crossing of the Atlantic. In a sense, nothing much happens. But the gruelling voyage is vividly brought to life, and we learn about the memories and hopes of the members of the Isaacs family and the other passengers, and their changing relationships. Between each chapter, there is a short passage of interior monologue presenting a character's thoughts.

Adèle Geras

The Fantora Family Files (1988)

The Fantoras are an extraordinary family. Filomena, the grandmother, can foretell the future by examining her knitting; her son Eddie can 'grow anything anywhere'; his wife Rosie knows how to fly; ten-year-old Bianca can bring things to life; nine-year-old Marco can make himself invisible; six-year-old Francesca can change the weather. But the most extraordinary member of the family by far is Ozymandias, the cat: 'the teller of stories, the Recounter of Family History, the Keeper of the Files'. This book consists of the stories which he tells about how his remarkable family deal with common situations like dancing classes, swimming, holidays, parties and cooking. The stories are linked by a connecting narrative and illustrated by extracts from the Files, for example, Auntie Varvara's Holiday Brochure, Marco's poem about moving, Francesca's party invitation. A very funny, utterly original book, with an unusual narrative structure and an even more unusual narrator!

In a sequel, *The Fantora Family Photographs* (1993), Ozymandias's stories are prompted by the family photographs hanging on the wall.

Golden Windows and Other Stories of Jerusalem (1995)

Harry, whose home is in New York, is visiting his Great Aunt Rachel in Jerusalem. A photograph that they look at together prompts Rachel to tell Harry a story involving the members of their family. Four more stories, quiet yet full of incident and memorable characters, follow. They are connected by a narrative which describes Harry's visit and the discussions he has with his aunt.

A Candle in the Dark (1995)

This story takes us back to Germany on the night of 9 November 1938. Gangs are smashing the windows of shops and houses belonging to Jews, and burning Jewish books. Clara and her little brother Maxie escape to a village in England. The gripping story is packed with vivid historical detail, and firmly based on actual events. Between December 1938 and August 1939, 10,000 children left Germany for England. Few ever saw their parents again.

Morris Gleitzman

Morris Gleitzman was born in Lincolnshire in 1953. He moved with his family to Australia when he was sixteen. Before becoming a full-time author, he wrote screen-plays for film and television, and worked as a newspaper journalist. He lives in Sydney and has two children.

As well as being very funny, Morris Gleitzman's novels introduce us to a cast of wonderfully strong and eccentric characters, and offer an odd but illuminating view of life. Mainly set in Australia, his stories include many words and phrases used in that country, for instance, 'chooks' for chicken, 'crook' for broken and useless, and 'arvo' for afternoon.

The Other Facts of Life (1985)

Twelve-year-old Ben is spending a lot of time in the bathroom. His parents think he is 'growing up' and worrying about 'the facts of life'. But it's not this at all: what troubles Ben is pollution, war, disaster and starvation. How can he and his family bear to live their happy, secure, well-fed lives when such things are going on? He decides to draw the state of the world to people's attention. His efforts include shaving his head, disrupting a barbecue and a sailing trip, sitting in his father's shop window with a string of sausages around his neck, and 'liberating' the chickens from a factory farm. This is a sharp, witty novel in which the author has great fun tricking the reader about what is happening. Although about serious issues, this book is tremendously entertaining.

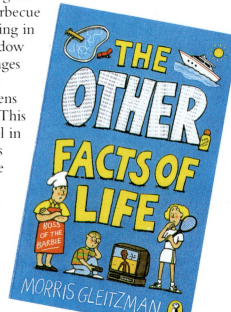

Morris Gleitzman

Misery Guts (1991)

Like all Morris Gleitzman's books, this one starts dramatically and memorably. Keith Shipley is painting his parents' fish and chip shop orange – Tropical Tango Hi-Gloss to be exact. It is his latest attempt to cheer them up, but like all the others, it fails. They explain to him that the fish and chip shop is not doing well, that they are short of money, and above all that they are disappointed because they have failed in their ambition to sell only the best quality fish and chips. Cheerful, ever-optimistic Keith refuses to give up. He decides that his parents must leave grey, rainy England and move to Paradise. This funny, compelling book describes how he brings this about.

Misery Guts has two equally funny sequels, both of them about Keith's continued attempts to solve his parents' problems. In *Worry Warts* (1992), he decides that what they need is wealth, and goes mining for precious jewels. In *Puppy Fat* (1995), his efforts shift to making them slim and beautiful.

Blabbermouth (1992)

Rowena Batts makes quite an entrance at her new school. Because she cannot speak, she introduces herself to the class with a friendly letter. This seems to be well-received, but when the teacher leaves the room, Darryn Peck begins to tease her. She puts up with this for a while, but when he says her parents must be freaks, she loses her temper, picks a frog out of the classroom tank, stuffs it in his mouth, winds sticky tape around his head, runs off and locks herself in the stationery cupboard. The arrival of her father to sort out the trouble makes things even worse. He is dressed as a cowboy and soon begins singing a Country and Western song – very badly. Strange, hilarious events follow thick and fast as Rowena gets to know her new school and tries to keep her father under control. She tells the story herself, and one of its delights is sharing her sharp, witty view of the world.

The sequel, *Sticky Beak* (1993), also opens memorably and messily when Rowena throws a Jelly Custard Surprise into a fan at the farewell party for her teacher, who has just married Rowena's father. What's even worse is that she cannot explain why she did it. Problems mount up for Rowena when she becomes the owner of a foul-mouthed cockatoo, and her father continues to be a painful embarrassment. The story fizzes with humour from start to finish.

Gene Kemp

Gene Kemp was born in a village near Tamworth in Staffordshire. She now lives in Devon in the house where her mother grew up. She has taught in both primary and secondary schools. She took up a career as a writer after her first novel, *The Turbulent Term of Tyke Tyler*, won the Carnegie Prize.

Gene Kemp is best known for her novels about Cricklepit Combined School. Each of the books in this series has its own very distinctive qualities.

The Turbulent Term of Tyke Tyler (1977)

Tyke Tyler is always getting into trouble of one kind or another, but is very loyal where friendship is involved. This story tells of Tyke's attempts to prevent Danny being sent off to a special school – attempts which include stealing test papers and finally, on the last day of term, climbing the bell tower and defiantly ringing the school bell. An exciting, amusing, moving story, full of surprises – and the biggest surprise of all is kept to the very end.

Gowie Corby Plays Chicken (1979)

Gowie Corby, a bully and a thief, is an outcast at Cricklepit Combined School – until he meets Rosie, an American girl who has moved in next door, and who makes a habit of turning up to rescue him from trouble. Their developing friendship is at the centre of this realistic, hard-edged story, which again has a surprise at the end. Told by the adult Gowie Corby, the story has an interesting and unusual structure.

Gene Kemp

The Clock Tower Ghost (1981)

A family decide to set up a museum in an old tower. However, they do not realise that it is haunted not by just one ghost but by two: one, a rich and pompous lord who apparently committed suicide there; the other, a crow shot down at the Battle of Hastings. The funniest parts of this very amusing story come when these two ghosts encounter Mandy, the truly vile daughter of the family.

Charlie Lewis Plays for Time (1984)

This intriguing story revolves around the relationship between two children, both at Cricklepit Combined, but from very different families: Trish, a member of the large and turbulent Moffat family, and Charlie, who lives an apparently quiet, comfortable and elegant life with his mother, a famous pianist.

Jason Bodger and the Priory Ghost (1985)

A nervous student teacher takes the class on an outing to a nearby priory. There, Jason Bodger, the class troublemaker, mysteriously encounters Mathilda de Chetwynde, a girl from 700 hundred years ago, and gets more caught up in history than he had bargained for. A funny, light-hearted story which is a joy to read from its very first sixteen-line sentence that mirrors the shape of a crocodile line of children. The footnotes offer witty advice, for example, just before a long description of a forest: 'Get through as quick as poss, so you can read the good bits'.

Juniper: a Mystery (1986)

Juniper Cantello feels secure and happy at Cricklepit Combined School, but she is troubled by nightmares. One involves events from 'The Juniper Tree', a folk tale by the Brothers Grimm. As a young child, Juniper had loved this story because her name came into it. Now, it seems to be telling her disturbing things about her own life.

Just Ferret (1990)

Ferret's first day at Cricklepit Combined is filled with anxieties and alarms. He can't read very well, and he is upset by the bullying that goes on in the school – upset not only because he is bullied himself, but because he feels deeply that bullying is wrong. He decides to take action to end it. Each chapter in this tense, realistic story is headed by a joke or saying.

Dick King-Smith

After service in the Second World War, in which he was seriously wounded, Dick King-Smith took up farming. This was not successful, and he tried several other jobs before starting to train as a teacher at the unusually advanced age of fifty. He spent seven years as a teacher in a primary school, writing stories during the holidays. He is now a prolific and successful author.

The Mouse Butcher (1981)

This is a darker, more hard-edged novel than most by Dick King-Smith. After a terrible storm, the human inhabitants of an island flee, taking their dogs with them but leaving their cats behind. Gradually, these cats take on the personalities and roles of their previous owners (butcher, vicar, shop owner, lord of the manor...) and form their own society. The story goes on to tell of the difficulties they face as the island becomes increasingly overgrown and derelict, and especially of the threat from a mutant cat as big as a dog. This world is vividly brought to life and there are some exciting and chilling moments as the plot unfolds.

The Sheep-pig (1983)

Farmer Hogget wins a piglet at the village show and names it Babe. It settles down to live with the sheep-dog Fly as its mother, starts copying her, and turns out to be wonderfully talented at herding sheep. Babe's unusual approach is to treat the sheep politely. This is a delightful novel full of charm, humour and excitement, with a compelling plot. *Babe*, the film version of the book, was an enormous hit in 1996.

A sequel to the book, *Ace* (1990), features Babe's great-grandson, another remarkable pig who masters human speech.

Dick King-Smith

Harry's Mad (1984)

When Harry learns that his eccentric Great Uncle George has left him something in his will, he imagines all kinds of extravagant things. When it turns out to be an African Grey Parrot called Madison, he is disappointed. However, this is no ordinary parrot: Mad, as he is known for short, can play the piano, is highly educated, and a great conversationalist. Harry is devastated when Mad disappears during a burglary at the house. But surely a parrot with his talents will find some way of getting back home? A warm, amusing story with two strong, interesting characters in Harry – and the parrot!

Lady Daisy (1992)

Unusually for Dick King-Smith, this is a story without animals. There is a non-human character, however: the Victorian doll, Lady Daisy, which Ned finds when clearing out the attic at his grandmother's house. When he picks it up, it opens its eyes and begins talking to him. Ned grows fond of the doll, which has a resolute, thoughtful character, and she tries hard to come to terms with the twentieth century. He learns a lot from looking after her, too, especially when he is bullied for taking her to school, and when she is stolen by an unscrupulous antique dealer. A tender, moving, rather sombre story.

Find the White Horse (1991)

Squintum, a cross-eyed Siamese cat, rescues Lubber, a large, slow-witted dog, from 'being put to sleep' at the dogs' home because no-one has come to claim him. Together, they set out to find Lubber's home, which he vaguely recalls was in a village where a white horse was carved in the chalk hillside. On the way they meet a racing pigeon, which has unhelpfully lost its sense of direction, and an Irish Setter, and the quartet have many adventures. These animal characters, with their human qualities, are appealing and well-drawn. Human characters, by comparison, play only a minor part. This is a funny, exciting story with some moments of sadness.

The Merrythought (1993)

Nick does not bother making the traditional wish when he gets the bigger part of the wishbone. Instead, he glues the two parts back together, and, remembering the words of his father, a vicar, makes an unselfish wish. It comes true. The wishbone continues to grant Nick's wishes, though not always quite in the way he had anticipated. The responsibility of being able to make things come true, and the possibility of misusing this power, begin to worry him. This is a fast-moving, warm-hearted story, which, like much of Dick King-Smith's work, is concerned with the right and decent way to behave.

Robert Leeson

Robert Leeson was born in Cheshire in 1928. At the age of sixteen he began working for a local newspaper, and returned to this career after he served in the Second World War. He started to write stories for his own children in the 1960s, and published his first novel in 1971.

Challenge in the Dark (1978)

During his first week at school, Mike Baxter gets into a confrontation with a new boy. In an attempt to resolve it, Mike issues a challenge: they should go down into the disused underground shelter nearby, and see who can stay there longer. They both become lost and frightened, help each other, and end up as friends. An exciting, gritty, realistic story told in Mike's own words.

Harold and Bella, and Jammy and Me (1980)

Seventeen very short stories about the adventures of a gang of children, mostly involving trouble of one kind or another, as they explore the local countryside and encounter various people. The four main characters are strongly drawn, and the stories provide an entertaining mixture of humour and excitement. They are told in the first-person by the 'me' of the title, and most begin with a traditional rhyme.

Third Class Genie (1979)
Genie on the Loose (1984)
The Last Genie (1993)

Third Class Genie is a lively, fast-moving and very funny story in which anything can happen – and usually does.

Robert Leeson

Alec keeps a mental score of his triumphs and disasters. The Monday on which the story begins looks like bringing nothing but disasters, including one in the form of the school bully. Escaping from him to an area of waste ground, Alec finds a sealed but apparently empty beer can with a label he has never seen before. When he opens it later, there is a rush of air and a voice thundering his name: it is a genie, who introduces himself as Abu Salem, Genie of the Third Order. He adopts Alec as his master, and, like all good genies, promises to do whatever his master commands. All sorts of hilarious and unlikely adventures follow as, with the genie's help, Alec tries to increase his score of triumphs. The trouble is that the magic of third class genies does not always work quite as intended.

Robert Leeson followed this novel with two sequels. In *Genie on the Loose*, Alec releases Abu Salem's son, Abdul, from the beer can. Abdul, unfortunately, is only an apprentice genie, and his attempts at magic are even more disastrous than his father's. *The Last Genie* finds Alec hoping for a quiet life. But instead he is swept off on a flying bed across the Sahara to the cities and palaces of the Middle East, and finds himself in desperate need of help.

The Zarnia Experiment series

This is a sequence of six science fiction novels organised in phases: Phase 1, *Landing* (1991); Phase 2, *Fire!* (1991); Phase 3, *Deadline* (1992); Phase 4, *Danger Trail* (1993); Phase 5, *Hide and Seek* (1993); and Phase 6, *Blast Off!* (1993). They tell the story of four children who get caught up in an experiment being carried out on Earth by robots from the planet Zarnia. Packed with adventures and ideas, The Zarnia Experiment series is one of the few successful attempts at science fiction for children. It will take the reader into a future world which is recognisable, yet strange and full of surprises.

Swapper (1994)

This short, illustrated novel is not as simple as it might seem at first. Stephen, known as Swapper, has turned swapping into a business. Scott thinks that he can outdo him, and invents the ingenious rolling swap in an attempt to get the hand-held computer game that he wants. This plan quickly runs out of control as he loses his best friend, and is tempted to swap things that belong to his sick grandfather. What starts out as a simple story of playground rivalry becomes a moving and thought-provoking story about the truly valuable things in life that cannot be swapped. As in much of Robert Leeson's work, there is at the heart of this story a deep concern with moral values and human relationships.

Jan Mark

Jan Mark was born in the village of Welwyn in Hertfordshire. She studied at art college in Canterbury and taught for a while in a secondary school. After marrying, she moved to Norfolk, which is the setting for several of her books. She now lives in Oxford, where she has worked as writer-in-residence with students training to be teachers.

Character, dialogue and setting, rather than action, are the keynotes of Jan Mark's work. Her subtle, witty, compassionate stories give us new ways of looking at life.

Thunder and Lightnings (1975)

Jan Mark found instant acclaim with this, her first novel, which won the Carnegie Medal. The Lightnings of the title are planes, and Victor, who lives near the RAF base from which they fly, knows everything there is to know about them. He is a strange, solitary child, but sharing his enthusiasm for the planes with Andrew, the new boy in the village, is the beginning of the close friendship at the centre of this novel. A moving, perceptive story about relationships, growing up and school life. Notice Victor's ingenious strategy for coping with project work!

Nothing to be Afraid Of (1980)

Do not believe this title. There is definitely something to be afraid of in these stories – in particular, an assortment of remarkably unsavoury characters, all too vividly described. Gritty, realistic stories with surprise endings which keep the reader in scary suspense all the way through.

Hairs in the Palm of Your Hand (1981)

How much time can you waste at school in a week? What happens if you turn up at a school pretending to be a new pupil? These questions are answered in the two stories in

Jan Mark

this book. Both are subversive, fast-moving and full of realistic dialogue. As in well-told jokes, things fall into place only at the very end.

Handles (1983)

This story, which also won the Carnegie Medal, opens the reader's eyes to other lives and other places, and other ways of seeing the world.

Eleven-year-old Erica Timperley is packed off to spend the summer holidays in a remote Fenland village with her aunt and uncle and her appallingly rude and lazy cousin. Her boredom ends when she discovers the motorcycle repair shop – a place that becomes for her a magical kingdom. There she meets an assortment of eccentric people, each of whom has his or her own witty and appropriate handle – or nickname. For instance, there are The Gremlin, Kermit, Bunny and Yerbut (who begins every sentence with the words 'Yer, but...'). Eventually, just before she has to leave, Erica gets her own handle.

This story is full of fascinating characters, and the wide, flat landscapes of East Anglia are vividly described. Memorable phrases and images (for instance, a peacock landing in the garden 'like a dozy paratrooper in evening dress') make it a delight to read.

Finders, Losers (1990)

In this intriguing and original collection of six linked short stories, Jan Mark explores the idea that 'Most of the things that happen to us happen because of something that somebody else has done. And in the same way, the things that we do make something happen for someone else.' The stories are all set on the same day on the same street, and involve six children who, though they may not know it, affect each others lives. The stories can be read in any order – but only when they have all been read can the reader see the full picture and understand what has happened and why.

A Fine Summer Knight (1995)

Grace, the youngest member of a large family, is always being told that she is not old enough; she feels sometimes that she never will be. One day she looks through a telescope and sees what she takes to be the ghost of a knight in armour on a distant hillside. Going in search of it, she finds things that are even more interesting: a guardian angel and a real live army of knights. This is a rich, multi-layered story with a very modern feel. It offers a fascinating picture of a child moving out from her family into the wider world, and raises interesting questions about the relationship between past and present.

Graham Oakley

Graham Oakley has worked as a designer for BBC Television and the Royal Opera House in London. He lives in a converted water mill in Wiltshire.

His books are dominated by large, detailed, action-packed pictures which do much more than just illustrate the text in the usual way: the reader has to look at them carefully to make sense of what is happening. As well as being very funny, his sophisticated stories are thought-provoking and satirical. Graham Oakley loves to poke fun at modern technology and at what he sees as pompous or silly behaviour.

The Church Mice series

Graham Oakley is best known for this series of ten books which he began in 1972 with *The Church Mouse*. The mice live in Wortlethorpe church. So does Sampson, the church cat, who has listened to so many sermons about loving your neighbour that he is determined to live peaceably with the mice no matter how much they try his patience. Each book tells the story of a different event which disrupts the lives of cat and mice. For example, in *The Church Mice Adrift* (1976) there is an invasion of rats, and capture by space scientists features in *The Church Mice and the Moon* (1974).

Hetty and Harriet (1981)

Hetty and Harriet are discontented chickens who decide to leave the farm and move to the place 'just over there' where everything is perfect. When it turns out to be far from perfect, they set off again. Each move takes them to a place more desperate and dangerous than the last, until they end up in a nightmarish meat-processing factory from which they are lucky to escape. This is a thought-provoking story about rural and urban life and the idea of progress.

Graham Oakley

Henry's Quest (1986)

This, perhaps Graham Oakley's darkest book, is set in a future in which modern technology has been wiped out. The king of this land has a vague memory that the cars in his museum once moved by themselves, and that this was connected with something called petrol. Obsessed with legends and fairy tales, he issues a proclamation that anyone who can discover this mysterious substance shall marry his daughter. Henry, a shepherd, takes up the challenge, and sets off on a journey through this strange and threatening world where people live in thatched jumbo jets, animals from abandoned safari parks roam wild, and great carts are propelled by sails.

Once Upon a Time: a Prince's Fantastic Journey (1990)

The modern world and the world of fairy tales exist together in this more light-hearted book. Accompanied by his page, Prince Alfred sets out to seek his fortune. He buys a car, and, disregarding traffic signs because they cannot be intended for royalty, turns down a 'funny little road' into a world where they meet Cinderella, Jack and the Giant, a cottage made of sweets, and many, many other characters, places and incidents from fairy tales. However, Prince Alfred does not know his fairy tales and gets everything wrong. The story is told by the prince's page, who, fortunately, is familiar with fairy tales, and provides a witty commentary on the action shown in the pictures.

The Foxbury Force (1994)
The Foxbury Force and the Pirates (1995)

There is not much crime in Foxbury, a sleepy town inhabited entirely by foxes. To provide practice for the local police force, the town council hires a firm of burglars to rob a shop once a month. The plan works well – until the burglars break the rules by keeping the loot. In *The Foxbury Force and the Pirates*, the police set out to arrest the pirates who are causing trouble on the municipal boating lake. Two funny, light-hearted stories, though with some sharp comments on the nature of crime, punishment and the law.

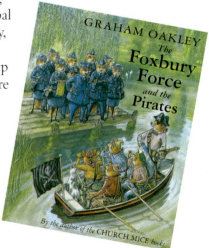

Philippa Pearce

Philippa Pearce was born in a village in Cambridgeshire in 1920. After going to Cambridge University, she became a Civil Servant. During the Second World War, she worked in the Schools Radio Department of the BBC as a scriptwriter and programme producer. This was followed by jobs in publishing, where she edited educational books and books for children.

Despite a relatively small output, Philippa Pearce is recognised as a major children's writer. Though delicate and reflective, her work has great imaginative power. The creation of imaginary worlds and the relationship between children and adults are two common themes in her stories.

The Minnow on the Say (1955)

This, her first novel, is a gentle adventure story about two boys who live by a river, go canoeing, and get involved in a treasure hunt. Philippa Pearce grew up in a water mill on the River Cam – a fact that may contribute to the story's vivid atmosphere and detail.

Tom's Midnight Garden (1958)

One of the most acclaimed children's novels of the century. Tom is staying with his aunt while his brother recovers from measles. Bored and restless, he gets up in the middle of the night, hears the clock strike thirteen, and steps back in time some 80 years, into a beautiful garden. He returns every night, and becomes involved in the lives of the people he meets there, especially young Hatty, who, he later discovers, is the old lady who lives in the flat above his aunt. This is a beautiful, slow-moving story, full of atmosphere and mystery.

Philippa Pearce

A Dog So Small (1970)

Here, Philippa Pearce continues to explore the boundaries between reality and fantasy. Ben is bitterly disappointed when the promised gift of a dog turns out to be not the real live thing but only an embroidered picture. Then he discovers that if he closes his eyes, this dog of fabric and thread becomes real – so real that it leads him into a road accident. As a result of this, Ben meets a real dog which his family allows him to keep. This is a story which takes the reader deep inside the world of a character's thoughts and feelings.

The Battle of Bubble and Squeak (1980)

This book is rather more direct and simple, and much shorter than *A Dog So Small*. Bubble and Squeak are gerbils, and the battle involves the Parker children's struggle to be allowed to keep them as pets and to come to terms with changes in their lives after their mother's re-marriage. The fast-moving, vividly written story is packed with emotional ups and downs, but is completely unsentimental in its portrayal of the characters and their relationships.

What the Neighbours Did (1972)

Philippa Pearce writes short stories as well as novels. This collection contains eight gentle, humorous stories about experiences and feelings that are easy to identify with, for example, overcoming a fear, trying to outwit adults.

The Shadow-Cage and Other Tales of the Supernatural (1978)

This is a challenging and chilling collection of ten stories about ghosts, visions, objects with sinister properties and other things supernatural. The stories are all the more scary and disturbing because the supernatural happenings take place in such ordinary settings, and because the author does not always show or explain what is going on. The reader is left wondering!

Philip Ridley

Although you might not immediately realise it, all Philip Ridley's stories are set in the East End of London, where he was born and still lives. He took up writing after a short but successful career as a painter. As well as stories for children, he has written adult novels, plays for stage and radio, and scripts for films, one of which he also directed himself.

His stories, a wonderful mixture of grimy realism and fantasy, are like modern fairy tales. The short episodes, swift descriptions, and emphasis on dialogue give his work the pace and style of films rather than conventional novels.

Dakota of the White Flats (1989)

A story full of extraordinary characters: Dakota's mother, who, since being abandoned by her husband, has not moved from her armchair and eats nothing but doughnuts; Lassiter Peach, a bestselling author who lives like a hermit on an island; Medusa, an out of work actress obsessed with jewellery. The no less extraordinary plot involves the search for a jewel-encrusted turtle brooch and the daring crossing of a river infested with ferocious mutant eels. A wildly inventive novel with cliff hanging chapter endings and lots of illustrations.

Krindlekrax (1991)

Thin, bespectacled Ruskin Spear dreams of being a hero. In reality, though, he is terrorised, like the other inhabitants of Lizard Street, by the bullying Elvis Cave who goes round smashing windows with his football. Ruskin gets a chance to prove himself when the fearsome Krindlekrax arises from the sewers beneath the street. An exciting and immensely satisfying story which shows that courage has nothing to do with size, or strength, or being aggressive.

Philip Ridley

Meteorite Spoon (1994)

What can Filly and Fergal Thunder do? Their parents argue more than any parents in The Whole History of Parents Arguing. The answer comes in the form of the meteorite spoon which an old lady wearing a bird's nest for a wig gives to them one day. Their parents' next argument is so violent that the house falls down. Filly and Fergal dig their way out of the rubble with the meteorite spoon, and find themselves transported to the island paradise of Honeymoonia. They see a happy, loving couple on the beach. Could it be their parents as they used to be? In *Meteorite Spoon,* as in many of Philip Ridley's books, it is children who show adults how to behave.

Kasper in the Glitter (1994)

Kasper lives with his mother, Pumpkin, in a beauty salon which now stands isolated and unused in the midst of waste ground. Theirs is a strange relationship. He looks after her; she keeps him to herself, shut up and friendless. All he knows about the world has been learned from magazines.

One night, Kasper meets Heartthrob Mink, who tells him about the city where he lives. In fact, about two cities: the Glitter, 'where people have got somewhere to snuggle up in', and the Gloom, 'the city full of people with nowhere to live'. Kasper is fascinated and pleased because he thinks he has found a friend at last. But in the morning he discovers that his mother's favourite brooch is missing: Heartthrob must have taken it. He sets off for the city to find him and recover the brooch. It is an overwhelming experience for Kasper. He encounters many adventures and many extraordinary characters: Skinnybones, Poodlecut, Hushabye Brightwing, and most important of all, King Streetwise. Can Kasper resist the king's dangerous temptations?

A lavishly illustrated novel with a fast-moving plot, and a style that sometimes reads almost like poetry.

Jon Scieszka

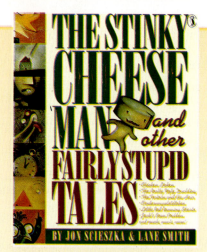

Jon Scieszka (pronounced Sheeska) was born in Michigan, USA, in 1954. He has had many different jobs, including painter, lifeguard and journalist on a magazine, and he began training to be a doctor. He now works as a primary school teacher and author.

In collaboration with the illustrator Lane Smith, he has created some of the strangest, most original and wildly imaginative children's books of the last few years. Lots of the fun comes from playing around with other stories and with the way books work.

The True Story of the 3 Little Pigs! (1989)

Here we learn from the wolf himself that 'the whole Big Bad Wolf thing is all wrong. The real story is about a sneeze and a cup of sugar'. And the misrepresentation is the fault of the newspapers who 'jazzed up the story'. This hilarious version of the well-known fairy tale is told in a slangy style ('Now the guy next door was a pig'), and the pictures and text are laid out in unusual and interesting ways.

The Frog Prince Continued (1991)

The author appears to tell the whole story in just one page: 'The princess kissed the frog. He turned into a prince. And they lived happily ever after'. Fortunately, however, that is not the end of this version of the story in which we learn that their life together was far from happy. This witty and provocative continuation of the well-known story has a real surprise at the end.

Jon Scieszka

The Stinky Cheese Man and other Fairly Stupid Tales (1992)

In this extraordinary book, Jon Scieszka transforms not just one fairy tale but a whole collection. For example, the Ugly Duckling grows up into – an ugly duck; the Gingerbread Man becomes the Stinky Cheese Man, who smells so bad that no-one wants to catch him. The author and illustrator also have lots of fun with the way books work and the way they look. The Little Red Hen tries to start telling her story before the title page and gets into an argument with Jack, the 'editor'. Jack later interrupts the first story because he has forgotten the Table of Contents, and then ruins the story of Little Red Running Shorts and ends up with a blank page. The dedication is printed upside down (it doesn't matter because no-one reads dedications anyway). A clever, witty book which offers something new and unexpected on every page.

The Time Warp Trio series

Joe's uncle, a magician, has given him a book of spells. With his friends, Fred and Sam, he uses this to travel into the past or the future. The trouble is that the spells do not always work exactly as the trio had intended. In *The Not-so-jolly Roger* (1991) they look up 'treasure', and are whisked back in time to a desert island where they become the prisoners of the desperate and dangerous pirate, Captain Blackbeard. In *Your Mother Was a Neanderthal* (1993) they go back to the Stone Age, taking with them such modern inventions as personal stereos and water pistols, and facing the dangers of dinosaurs and woolly mammoths. In *The Knights of the Kitchen Table* (1991) they return to the reign of King Arthur, and in *The Good, the Bad and the Goofy* (1992), to the Wild West.

This is a series of short novels in which the text and the many strange, zany pictures work very closely together. The action unfolds at a furious pace, with lots of humour based on the clash between different periods of time. There is also plenty of word play – including terrible jokes and puns!

Maths Curse (1995)

A girl wakes up one day to find herself in a world where everything is (as her teacher had said) a maths problem. She finally breaks free of this curse – only to wake up the following day in a world where everything is a science experiment. A fascinating and original book which offers not just a story, but also lots of things to puzzle over and investigate.

Jill Paton Walsh

Jill Paton Walsh was born in London, where she also went to school. After studying English Literature at Oxford University, she taught English in a girls' school before taking up a career as an author. She has three children, and now lives in Cambridge. She owns a narrow boat, and her family take holidays on the canals. She has written novels for a wide age range, from young children to teenagers and adults. Most of her books have an historical setting.

Fireweed (1969)

Set during the Second World War, this is the story of two young teenagers, Bill and Julie, who have escaped back to London after being evacuated to the country. It tells of their strange, dangerous, furtive existence in the bombed city, and of their increasingly close and dependent relationship. Told in the first person by Bill, the story is tense and atmospheric with moments of real excitement and sadness. Life at the time of the Blitz is vividly recreated, and there is a large cast of fascinating minor characters. A challenging novel with a very adult tone.

The Butty Boy (1975)

Eleven-year-old Harriet, the child of a wealthy family, is lonely and unhappy at the new home to which they have just moved. One day, she sees a narrow boat gliding past on the canal at the bottom of the garden. Impulsively, she runs after it and is taken on board by the two children who are piloting it. Before she knows what is happening, she finds herself helping them to deliver their cargo of coal on time – a journey which introduces her to a new world. A warm, sensitive story, full of exact and fascinating historical detail about life at the end of the nineteenth century. It is

Jill Paton Walsh

told by Kate, the eleven-year-old cousin of the now adult Harriet, and from her we learn how the canal adventure changed Harriet's life for ever.

Gaffer Samson's Luck (1984)

When James moves with his family from Yorkshire to a village in the Norfolk Fens, he finds that their neighbour is an old man called Gaffer Samson. A close relationship forms between the two of them, and when Gaffer Samson becomes ill, he asks James to go and fetch his 'luck': a black stone in the shape of a leaf given to him in his youth by a gypsy woman. Will James find the stone before Gaffer Samson dies? Is it just an ordinary stone, or does it, as the gypsy woman said, have special powers? A sub-plot involves James's gradual acceptance by the village children. The two strands are joined in a thrilling climax on the flooded Fens.

This novel of just a hundred or so pages combines exciting adventure with vivid descriptions of the countryside and sensitive portrayals of changing relationships.

Pepi and the Secret Names (1994)

This is a large format picture book with gloriously coloured illustrations by Fiona French, in the style of Ancient Egyptian paintings. Pepi's father, who is painting the walls of the tomb being built for Prince Dhutmose, likes to work with live subjects. This presents no problem when he wants to paint geese, but what about lions, hawks and snakes? Pepi solves the problem by discovering the secret names of these animals. When he calls them by these names, they come willingly to the tomb for Pepi's father to paint them. Indeed, the snake is so keen to be painted that it *tells* Pepi its secret name. The names are given in Egyptian hieroglyphics and can be worked out by using the code at the end of the book.

A picture book which offers a powerful story and insights into the culture of Ancient Egypt.

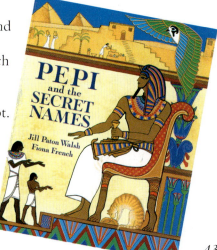

43

Jacqueline Wilson

Jacqueline Wilson was born in Bath in 1945, but spent most of her childhood in Kingston, Surrey, where she still lives. She has been writing stories since she was a child, and finished her first novel at the age of only nine. After a few years working with a publishing company and as a magazine journalist, she took up a career as an author. Although best known as a writer of books for children, she has also written crime novels and radio plays for adults.

Take a Good Look (1990)

Mary felt 'as if she was stuck being a baby for ever just because she was nearly blind'. Deciding to do something for herself for once, she sets off to the local shop, and stumbles upon an armed robbery. When the police arrive, the robbers grab Mary and take her hostage. They cannot believe their luck when they realise that she won't be able to recognise them – but do not reckon with her bravery and resourcefulness. A tense, realistic novel with moments of real shock and violence. It has something to say about growing up and becoming independent for all children.

The Werepuppy (1991)

Left in the care of his older sisters one night, Micky watches a video featuring a werewolf. It frightens him badly, and he starts imagining werewolves everywhere – in his grandmother's old fox fur cape, and especially in every dog, no matter how gentle and harmless. To calm his fears, Micky's parents decide to get him a dog of his own. At the kennels, he chooses a puppy – or does it choose him? Either way, the two of them hit it off immediately, as if they both understood the purpose of it all, and Micky names the puppy Wolfie. A simple, funny, perceptive story about fears and overcoming them. There is a sequel, *The Werepuppy on Holiday* (1994).

Jacqueline Wilson

The Story of Tracy Beaker (1991)

Tracy lives in a children's home but desperately wants a proper home of her own. At the suggestion of her social worker, she starts to write her autobiography, and it is through this that the reader finds out about her hopes, her worries and her anger. Tracy knows that she can be difficult, and writes longingly of her mother whom she hopes will come to visit her. As in many of her books, Jacqueline Wilson offers humour and feeling in tackling the issue of a child in an unhappy situation.

The Suitcase Kid (1992)

When Andrea's parents split up, she feels as if she is being split up, too. They tell her that moving between their two homes will be as easy as ABC. It turns out to be much more complicated and stressful than that, especially when a new baby is born. Andrea copes with it all with the help of Radish, her toy rabbit and comforter. The lively story is told in the first person by Andrea herself, and is full of sharp observations. It is divided into short chapters with ABC titles: 'A is for Andy', 'B is for Bathroom', 'C is for Cottage'… 'Z is for Zoe'.

The Bed and Breakfast Star (1994)

This is an inviting, jolly-looking book with lots of small cartoon-style illustrations. These fit in closely with the text and are presented as if drawn by the narrator, Elsa. Named after the famous lion, and with hair like a lion's mane, Elsa counts out her life in beds: all the different beds that she has slept in during a life full of moves. As the story begins, the family has become homeless, and is forced to move into bed and breakfast accommodation. It is a desperate situation, but irrepressible, courageous Elsa does her best to keep the family's spirits up, although the adults do not always appreciate her jokes. Even more bravery and resourcefulness is called for when she discovers that the hotel is on fire. The story is told in Elsa's own words, in a quick, chatty style. Again, what could be a gloomy, depressing subject is treated with humour and optimism.

Title index

Angel of Nitshill Road, The, Anne Fine	17
Apprentices, The, Leon Garfield	20
Backlash, Nicholas Fisk	19
Battle of Bubble and Squeak, The, Philippa Pearce	37
Bed and Breakfast Star, The, Jacqueline Wilson	45
Blabbermouth, Morris Gleitzman	25
Black Hearts in Battersea, Joan Aiken	4
Black Jack, Leon Garfield	20
Blast Off (*The Zarnia Experiment* series), Robert Leeson	31
Blewcoat Boy, Leon Garfield	21
Blossom Family Library series, *The*, Betsy Byars	13
Blossom Promise, A (*The Blossom Family Library* series), Betsy Byars	13
Blossoms and the Green Phantom, The (*The Blossom Family Library* series), Betsy Byars	13
Blossoms Meet the Vulture Lady, The (*The Blossom Family Library*), Betsy Byars	13
Boat Girl (*Dockside School* series), Bernard Ashley	9
Break in the Sun, Bernard Ashley	8
Bridle the Wind, Joan Aiken	5
Broops! Down the Chimney, Nicholas Fisk	19
Butty Boy, The, Jill Paton Walsh	42
Bundle of Nerves, A, Joan Aiken	5
Candle in the Dark, A, Adèle Geras	23
Caretaker's Cat, The (*Dockside School* series), Bernard Ashley	9
Challenge in the Dark, Robert Leeson	30
Charlie Lewis Plays for Time, Gene Kemp	27
Church Mice series, Graham Oakley	34
Church Mice and the Moon, The (*Church Mice* series), Graham Oakley	34
Church Mice Adrift, The (*Church Mice* series), Graham Oakley	34
Church Mouse, The (*Church Mice* series), Graham Oakley	34
Clipper, Spag and Barny stories, Gillian Cross	14
Clock Tower Ghost, The Gene Kemp	27
Coast to Coast, Betsy Byars	13
Cold Shoulder Road, Joan Aiken	4
Computer Nut, The, Betsy Byars	13
Creepy Company, A, Joan Aiken	4
Crummy Mummy and Me, Anne Fine	16
Cuckoo Tree, The, Joan Aiken	4
Dakota of the White Flats, Philip Ridley	38
Danger Trail (*The Zarnia Experiment* series), Robert Leeson	31
Deadline (*The Zarnia Experiment* series), Robert Leeson	31
Demon Headmaster, The, Gillian Cross	15
Dido and Pa, Joan Aiken	4
Dockside School series, Bernard Ashley	9
Dog So Small, A, Philippa Pearce	37
The Eighteenth Emergency, Betsy Byars	13
Fantora Family Files, The, Adèle Geras	23
Fantora Family Photographs, The, Adèle Geras	23
Father Christmas, Raymond Briggs	10
Finders, Losers, Jan Mark	33
Find the White Horse, Dick King-Smith	29
Fine Summer Knight, A, Jan Mark	33
Fire! (*The Zarnia Experiment* series), Robert Leeson	31
Fireweed, Jill Paton Walsh	42
Fit of Shivers, A, Joan Aiken	5
Flour Babies, Anne Fine	17
Foxbury Force, The, Graham Oakley	35
Foxbury Force and the Pirates, The, Graham Oakley	35
Frog Prince Continued, The, Jon Scieszka	40
Fungus the Bogeyman, Raymond Briggs	10
Gaffer Samson's Luck, Jill Paton Walsh	43
Genie on the Loose, Robert Leeson	31
Gentleman Jim, Raymond Briggs	11
Getting In (*Dockside School* series), Bernard Ashley	9
Ghost of Dockside School, The (*Dockside School* series), Bernard Ashley	9
Girls in the Velvet Frame, The, Adèle Geras	22
Gobbo the Great (*Clipper, Spag and Barny* series), Gillian Cross	14
Goggle-Eyes, Anne Fine	16
Goose on Your Grave, A, Joan Aiken	5
Golden Windows and Other Stories of Jerusalem, Adèle Geras	23
Good, the Bad and the Goofy, The (*The Time Warp Trio* series) Jon Scieszka	41
Go Saddle the Sea, Joan Aiken	5
Gowie Corby Plays Chicken, Gene Kemp	26
Great Elephant Chase, The, Gillian Cross	15
Grinny, Nicholas Fisk	18
Hairs in the Palm of Your Hand, Jan Mark	32
Handles, Jan Mark	33
Harp of Fishbones, A, Joan Aiken	5

Title index

Harold and Bella, and Jammy and Me, Robert Leeson	30
Harry's Mad, Dick King-Smith	29
Henry's Quest, Graham Oakley	35
Hetty and Harriet, Graham Oakley	34
Hide and Seek (The Zarnia Experiment series), Robert Leeson	31
Hunky Parker Is Watching You, Gillian Cross	15
I'm Trying to Tell You, Bernard Ashley	9
Is, Joan Aiken	4
Jason Bodger and the Priory Ghost, Gene Kemp	27
Juniper: A Mystery, Gene Kemp	27
Just Ferret, Gene Kemp	27
Kasper in the Glitter, Philip Ridley	39
King in the Garden, The, Leon Garfield	21
King Nimrod's Tower, Leon Garfield	21
Knights of the Kitchen Table, The (The Time Warp Trio series) Jon Scieszka	41
Lady Daisy, Dick King-Smith	29
Landing (The Zarnia Experiment Series), Robert Leeson	31
Last Genie, The, Robert Leeson	31
Man, The, Raymond Briggs	11
Maths Curse, Jon Scieszka	41
Merrythought, The, Dick King-Smith	29
Meteorite Spoon, Philip Ridley	39
Midnight Fox, The, Betsy Byars	12
Minnow on the Say, The, Philippa Pearce	36
Mintyglo Kid, The (Clipper, Spag and Barny series), Gillian Cross	14
Misery Guts, Morris Gleitzman	25
Monster Maker, Nicholas Fisk	18
Mouse Butcher, The, Dick King-Smith	28
Mysteries of Harris Burdick, The, Chris van Allsburg	6
Night Birds on Nantucket, Joan Aiken	4
Nothing to be Afraid Of, Jan Mark	32
Not-just-anybody Family, The, (Blossom Family Library series), Betsy Byars	13
Not-so-jolly Roger, The (The Time Warp Trio series) Jon Scieszka	41
Once Upon a Time: A Prince's Fantastic Journey, Graham Oakley	35
Other Facts of Life, The, Morris Gleitzman	24
Pepi and the Secret Names, Jill Paton Walsh	43
Polar Express, The, Chris van Allsburg	7
Prime Minister's Brain, The, Gillian Cross	15
Puppy Fat, Morris Gleitzman	25
Rag, a Bone and a Hank of Hair, A, Nicholas Fisk	19
Revenge of the Demon Headmaster, The, Gillian Cross	15
Save Our School (Clipper, Spag and Barny series), Gillian Cross	14
Seeing Off Uncle Jack, Bernard Ashley	9
Shadow-Cage, The, Philippa Pearce	37
Sheep-pig, The, Dick King-Smith	28
Snowman, The, Raymond Briggs	11
Step by Wicked Step, Anne Fine	17
Sticky Beak, Morris Gleitzman	25
Stinky Cheese Man and Other Fairly Stupid Tales, The, Jon Scieszka	41
Stolen Lake, The, Joan Aiken	4
Story of Tracy Beaker, The, Jacqueline Wilson	45
Suitcase Kid, The, Jacqueline Wilson	45
Summer of the Swans, The, Betsy Byars	10
Swapper, Robert Leeson	29
Sweetest Fig, The, Chris van Allsburg	41
Swimathon (Clipper, Spag and Barny series), Gillian Cross	12
Talking Car, The, Nicholas Fisk	17
Take a Good Look, Jacqueline Wilson	44
Teeth of the Gale, The, Joan Aiken	5
Terry on the Fence, Bernard Ashley	6
Third Class Genie, Robert Leeson	28
Thunder and Lightnings, Jan Mark	30
Time Warp Trio series, The, Jon Scieszka	39
Tom's Midnight Garden, Philippa Pearce	34
Touch of Chill, A, Joan Aiken	5
True Story of the 3 Little Pigs, The, Jon Scieszka	38
Turbulent Term of Tyke Tyler, The, Gene Kemp	24
Voyage, Adèle Geras	20
Werepuppy, The, Jacqueline Wilson	44
What the Neighbours Did, Philippa Pearce	35
Whisper in the Night, A, Joan Aiken	5
Widow's Broom, The, Chris van Allsburg	7
Wolves of Willoughby Chase, The, Joan Aiken	4
Worry Warts, Morris Gleitzman	23
Wreck of the Zephyr, The, Chris van Allsburg	40
Writing on the Wall, The, Leon Garfield	19
Your Mother was a Neanderthal (Time Warp Trio series), Jon Scieszka	39
Zarnia Experiment series, The, Robert Leeson	29

Finding out more

Public libraries
The best source of (free!) books – and information. Just browse the shelves, or ask for help. One of the librarians is likely to have special responsibility for children's books. Find out who the person is, and ask them what's new and what they recommend. Tell them about the kind of books you like and what you've just been reading – and ask them to suggest something. There will probably also be leaflets from publishers and other organisations to look through.

Book shops
A book shop with a children's department will have a good selection of books currently available. Many now have a carpeted area or a few chairs where you can browse in comfort (for a while!) before you buy. A member of staff should be able to look up information about particular authors or titles on a computer, using the 'books in print' database. Some of the big book shop chains now operate a mail order catalogue service, which is especially useful if it is difficult for you to get to a good shop.

Magazines
Although most of the magazines about children's books are aimed at adults, at least some sections, especially the book reviews, are useful and interesting for children, too. You might find them in your school or in the local library.

Books for Keeps
B*f*K as it is familiarly known, bills itself as 'the largest circulation, wholly independent children's book review magazine now published in the UK for those who want children to know the pleasure and power of books'. Published six times a year, it provides reviews of fiction and non-fiction organised according to age ranges, articles about various aspects of children's books, news, and features about authors. B*f*K also publishes collections of reviews in book form. These include *The BfK Green Guide to Children's Books*, *A Multicultural Guide to Children's Books 0-12*, and *Poetry 0-16*.

Books for Your Children
This magazine, published three times a year, is intended for parents. Like *Books for Keeps*, it provides a mixture of features and reviews.

Carousel: the Guide to Children's Books
A colourful new magazine, also published three times a year. The reviews are organised according to reading ability rather than age.

In Brief
Published three times a year by Waterstones book shops, and available free at the time of publication from their shops. An independent guide, aimed mainly at teenagers, with reviews and author interviews.

Books about children's books
Again, these books are written with an adult audience in mind, but also provide interesting and useful information for children.

The Oxford Companion to Children's Literature
edited by Humphrey Carpenter and Maxi Pritchard (Oxford University Press)
An alphabetically organised reference book with entries on authors, titles, characters from books, and fictional genres (e.g. science fiction, westerns, fairy stories).

Meet the Authors and Illustrators: 60 Creators of Favourite Children's Books
by Stephanie Nettell (Scholastic)
Biographical articles about these authors and illustrators, focusing on how they became writers and how they go about writing. Also contains lists of selected titles.

Waterstones' Guide to Children's Books
This attractively illustrated and presented spiral-bound guide contains very short annotations of books, organised in sections according to age range from Pre-school to Young Adults. There is also information about some authors and a useful subject index.

A Book a Day Keeps the Boredom Away
(Cambridgeshire Libraries Publications Group)
The 365 books in this guide were actually chosen by children who participated in Cambridgeshire Libraries' Carnival of Books event in 1994. The short annotations, however, have been written by adults, and are organised into subject matter.

Hooked on Books by Chris Lutrario and John Hook (HarperCollins)
Written for teachers, this ringbinder contains detailed annotations of over 300 books for children of 9, 10 and 11 years of age. The entries are organised in four sections according to the type of book (Novels, Picture books, Collections of short stories, and Books in series), each subdivided into three sections according to how challenging they are to read. The 41 subject indexes will be especially useful.